The Character Builder's Bible

Tyndale House Publishers, Inc.

Carol Stream, Illinois

Old Testament Stories

New Testament Stories

About this book

No matter what your goal is in raising your children, they will have a greater chance of being happy and successful as they grow up if they learn good character traits from God's Word.

All Scripture is inspired by God and is useful to teach us what is true and to make us realize what is wrong in our lives. It corrects us when we are wrong and teaches us to do what is right.
2 Timothy 3:16

Note to parents and caregivers

These Bible stories are intended to help children identify important moral character traits as well as recognize how God reveals Himself to them.

Because we have tried to cover a wide range of topics, you will notice that each story focuses on a single one. But as you converse with your children, we invite you to dig deeper and mine further lessons in these Bible stories as is appropriate for their age.

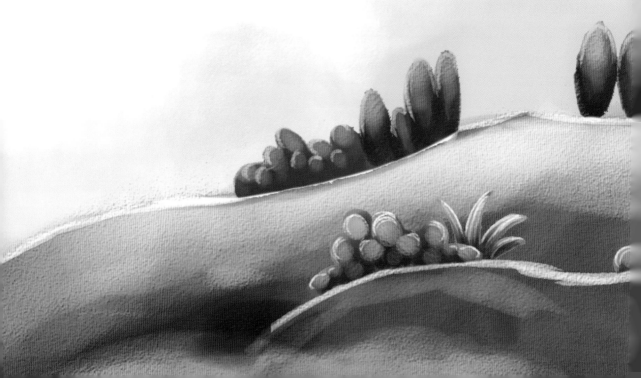

....

Presented to

....

From

....

Date

Lazy people are soon poor;
hard workers get rich.

Proverbs 10:4

God Makes the World

from Genesis 1

In the very beginning nothing existed except God. There were no shining stars, no cuddly animals, and no sweet-smelling flowers. There were not even people like you and me.

So God decided to make the world and fill it with beautiful plants, the most interesting creatures, and two amazing people.

"All done!" God said. "I like the way it came out. And it's now ready to be enjoyed!"

When we look at everything from the tallest mountain to the tiniest ant, it is simply amazing to think about how God was so diligent in every detail.

Diligence

Diligence means to do a good job
and keep going until you're done.
Yay! I was careful and thorough,
and I even had lots of fun!

8

My Mini Creations

When I bake cookies, I combine the right ingredients and shape them to perfection.

After baking comes my favorite part: decorating! I put on some icing, sprinkles, and nuts.

God had so many ideas for decorating His creations. He put stripes on zebras and polka dots on ladybugs.

Before I enjoy my creations, I take time to clean, wipe, and put things away.

Guard your heart
above all else.

Proverbs 4:23

The First Sin

from Genesis 3:1-6

The first people God made were called Adam and Eve. "I've created everything in this garden for you to enjoy: puppies and kittens, lions and bears, even apples and pomegranates. And, oh yes, don't forget the vegetables," God told them. Speaking of food, they could pick and eat from every tree in the garden, except one.

Things were going along quite nicely in the perfect place that God had made. But one day the sneaky devil came to Adam and Eve and said, "The fruit from this tree that God told you not to eat is delicious! You don't know what you're missing!"

They were tempted. It sure looked good! "Maybe just a small bite," they thought. CRUNCH! MUNCH!

Oops! That was a very sad choice, and this first sin separated people from God.

Self-Control

I control myself when I'm tempted to do
the things that I shouldn't do.
I turn around and walk away
before I say something untrue.

Difficult Situations

Ow! I ate too much dessert.
Now my tummy hurts.

Oh no! I spent all my money, and
now I don't have enough to buy my
friend a birthday gift.

It's not easy to control myself
in some of these situations.

So I ask God to help me
control my actions.

Do what is right and
good in the Lord's sight.

Deuteronomy 6:18

Following God

from Genesis 6:13-22

Many years and many people later, almost everyone had forgotten about God, and they were hurting one another. God found one man who loved to obey Him. His name was Noah. "I want to clean this world with a flood of water to start over," God said to Noah. "For that we're going to need a big boat, an ark."

"What's a boat? What's an ark?" Noah asked. "Is it supposed to be round like a bowl or square like a box?" If the ark was too heavy or had a leak, it would sink. If it was too flimsy, it would fall apart. So God gave Noah clear instructions on how to make the ark strong and big enough to fit Noah's family, two of each kind of animal, and lots of food for the trip.

They were saved from the flood because Noah did exactly what God told him to do.

Obedience

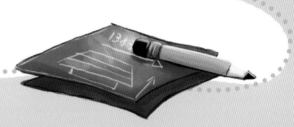

Obedience means to listen well
to whatever Mom and Dad say.
Whatever it is they want me to do,
I get it done right away.

My Brand-New Toy

My new Lego set! Whoopee!
But so many instructions?
I don't have time for this.

Later: This sure looks funny.
I think I'll start over and follow
the instructions.

It was important to follow the instructions because it helped
me to get it just right. Now, on to my next building project . . .

God opposes the
proud but gives grace
to the humble.

James 4:6

The Tall Tower

from Genesis 11:1-9

"Let's take sticks and bricks and build a big tower to show our power!" the people said. "Pass the bricks this way!" and "Lower the sticks that way!" they said to each other.

The higher the tower became, the more the people bragged. "This tower will show everyone how great we are!" they boasted. "We don't need God anymore."

That's not a good thing to say, and God didn't like it. So He mixed up their words. They began to talk in different languages and could not understand each other any longer. "Danky doodley day, zonky donko quay," was their new plan.

Nothing worked this way. God could not bless their project when they were not humble, so they never finished it.

Humility

I know that I'm not good enough.
I shouldn't brag or boast.
Humility is knowing that
I need God's help the most.

At Dance Practice

"I'm best at this! I don't need your suggestions."
Whoops! She's going her own way and turning away from God's plan.

"I'm sorry, you did have a good idea. Let's give it a try!"
God loves humility: putting others before ourselves and not getting puffed up.

Show me the right path, O Lord;
point out the road for me to follow.

Psalm 25:4

Abraham Relies on God

from Genesis 11:31–12:9

One day God spoke to Abraham and said, "Leave your home. I will show you a new land to travel to. Just follow My lead." So Abraham packed his bags and followed step by step as he took his family on a long trip.

It wasn't easy for Abraham to move so far away without even a car or train to help him. Instead, he had to walk and carry everything with him.

"I don't even know where we'll end up. It's like walking with a blindfold on. But I do know that I can count on God," Abraham thought. "Here we are!" God said. Abraham looked around and was pleased. "This place is great and so much better than the last!" Abraham built an altar to thank God for leading him and his family to this beautiful place. It pays to trust God.

Dependence on God

I depend on God when I follow Him
and trust the way He leads.
His choices are always best for me.
He provides for all my needs.

Changes and Changes

Our lives are full of changes.
We're moving to a new house, and I'll
have to make new friends.

Oh no, we missed our flight!
What will we do for vacation now?

My friend got sick, and now we can't
have a sleepover. I'm not happy
about this at all.

But I can always depend on God.
He never lets me down or
breaks a promise.

Wait patiently for the Lord. Be brave and courageous. Yes, wait patiently for the Lord.

Psalm 27:14

Waiting for a Baby

from Genesis 15–17, 21

Abraham and his wife, Sarah, had prayed for many years to have a baby. God promised to give them a big family. But now they were too old. "Did God forget about us, or did He change His mind?" they wondered.

Abraham didn't get impatient and say, "Hey, God! I think it's about time that You kept Your promise! Why haven't You given me a son already?" He continued to wait for God's answer, even though it took years.

When Abraham was 99 years old, God finally said, "NOW you will have a baby!" Abraham and Sarah named their miracle baby boy "Isaac," which means "laughter." They were so happy. They sang him songs, cuddled him, and taught him about God's goodness.

Patience

Patience is waiting for God's best time
when I want things right away.
I know that waiting helps me grow
more like Him every day.

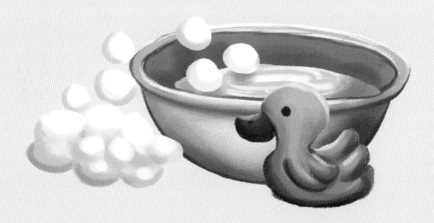

My Gardening Adventure

When I plant a seed, it doesn't grow in one hour or one day.

I can't even use a remote control to make it grow faster.

God takes His time to make the flower bloom beautifully . . .

. . . and it takes patience for my character to be beautiful too.

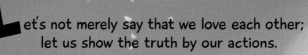

Let's not merely say that we love each other;
let us show the truth by our actions.

1 John 3:18

A Wife for Isaac

from Genesis 24

Abraham said to his son, "Isaac, it's time that you got married! But the right woman is not around here. I will send my trusted servant to my homeland to find you a wife." When the servant arrived he thought, "Oh my! What a difficult job. How will I know who the right one is?"

A woman named Rebekah came to the well to fill her water pot. "Would you like some water to drink? Should I also give your camels some water?" she asked. "Yes! She must be the one for Isaac!" thought the servant.

Rebekah gave him a drink and then pulled up buckets and buckets full of water for the camels. That was a lot of work because camels drink a lot of water. She saw the need and acted on it.

Initiative

I do the things that need to be done
even before Mom or Dad asks.
I look for opportunities
to help others in their tasks.

I'm Hungry

My tummy sure is growling after all that schoolwork.

Dad's out working, and Mom's quite busy. Looks like it could be a long wait to get a snack.

I know! I can practice my cooking skills and prepare my own snack. That's taking initiative.

The Lord . . . delights in those
who tell the truth.

Proverbs 12:22

Jacob Cheats

from Genesis 27

When Isaac was very old and couldn't see well anymore, he called his oldest son. "Esau! I want to bless you and give you all that I have, but first prepare me a meal." Esau went hunting for the meal.

While he was gone, his younger twin brother, Jacob, played a trick on him. He made his voice sound like Esau's and put goatskins on his arms to make them feel like his brother's.

Jacob brought a meal to his father and said, "I'm back. You can bless me now!" Isaac gave Jacob the blessing which he had meant for his older son. Esau came home to find out that Jacob had lied, cheated, and stolen the blessing. "I'm mad, very mad!" he shouted. "I'm scared, very scared!" said Jacob as he ran to another country. Being dishonest put him in a difficult situation.

Honesty

I say and do things
that are true and right.
Being trustworthy
is pleasing in God's sight.

Delicious Cookies?

These must be the new cookies
Mom made. Delicious!

Yum, yum, I want some! But the
sign says, "Do not eat!"

I want Mom to trust me,
so I'll just walk away.

Later: "Here, Rex, your doggie
biscuits," Mom says.

37

God arms me with strength,
and he makes my way perfect.

Psalm 18:32

A Special Dream

from Genesis 28:10-22

Jacob traveled until his feet ached. "It's getting dark, and I need a place to sleep. This rock will do for my pillow."

While Jacob slept, God gave him a dream of angels walking up and down a big stairway that reached all the way to heaven. God encouraged him and said, "I am watching over you, Jacob, and I will still bless you!"

Jacob woke up and said, "God has been with me, even when I didn't know it!" He took the rock that he had used as a pillow and set it up as a reminder of God's love and care even after he had cheated his brother.

Encouragement

God comforts me and helps me.
His words make my heart glad!
I can encourage others too
when they are feeling sad.

I Made a Mistake

Oops, I burned the toast! Mom's surprise breakfast is ruined.

Mom hugs me. "The eggs are delicious. I can tell that you worked hard making this."

"I'm sorry, Dad. I know not to run in the house." Dad still loves me and says, "I'll help you clean up, and then we can practice running outside instead."

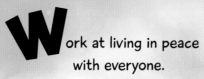

Work at living in peace
with everyone.
Hebrews 12:14

A Colorful Coat

from Genesis 37, 39–45

Jacob had 12 sons, but he liked Joseph the best. He gave him a colorful coat that made him look very handsome. "Why did he get a new coat, and we didn't? It's not fair!" his brothers complained.

They compared their things with Joseph's, and that made them feel grumpy. "We can't take it anymore! Let's tie him up and sell him as a slave." After many years of slavery and even prison, Joseph was made ruler of Egypt and given the important job of storing food for an upcoming famine.

Not long after, Joseph's brothers came with growling tummies to buy food in Egypt. There they saw Joseph, and even though he had a lot more than they did, it didn't matter anymore.

Joseph's love and forgiveness were worth more than anything they might envy.

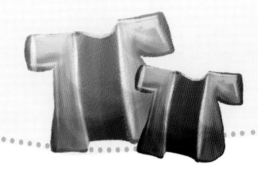

Comparing

When I compare, it's difficult
to enjoy God's many blessings.
I choose to be content instead
and thank Him for all things.

But I Only Have . . .

My brother just got a big new bike,
and I only have this little old wagon.

That's not fair. I want one too!

My brother just got a big new bike.
What could I do with my little wagon?

Yee-haw! I've got my very
own horse and chariot!

If you are faithful in little things,
you will be faithful in large ones.

Luke 16:10

A Helpful Sister

from Exodus 1:1–2:10

The new ruler of Egypt worried that God's people might get stronger than his people. "Throw all newborn baby boys into the river!" he said. What a crazy thing to do! Mothers thought so too! They hid their babies so that Pharaoh's soldiers couldn't find them.

One mother thought of a clever way to save her baby: she made a floating basket.

"I'll watch my baby brother," said Miriam. Miriam didn't let anything distract her from being a responsible sister to her little baby brother. She hid in the reeds as the basket rocked in the ripples. She kept a close watch from a distance.

The baby woke up. "WAAAH!" he cried. "What's that noise?" said the princess when she came to take a bath. "Don't cry! You'll be safe with me, and I'll name you Moses." Then Miriam interrupted. "Excuse me, miss. Do you need a nurse? I know the perfect one," she said and dashed off to get her mother.

Responsibility

I do what I'm supposed to do,
and I try to do it well.
That means that I am growing up,
can't you tell?

Brushing My Teeth

Brush, brush, brush!

Aren't those teeth
looking shiny clean?

We even brushed our teeth without being reminded.
That's one way we practice responsibility.

With God everything is possible.

Matthew 19:26

Crossing the Sea

from Exodus 3–14

When Moses grew up to be a man, God spoke to him. "The Israelites are treated terribly in Egypt. I want you to lead them out of here!" But Moses worried and said, "What do I say to the ruler? He won't agree." God reassured him. "Have faith in Me. I'll give you the words to say."

As Moses expected, the ruler did not agree. "No! I don't have to listen to you! I am the boss around here!" God allowed terrible disasters to happen to Egypt until the king changed his mind. "We are free! Let's go!" said the Israelites. But the Red Sea was in front of them. "The Egyptians are chasing us. We're in trouble!" they cried. "Don't worry!" Moses called out. "God will save us!"

WHOOOSH! With a huge wind God pushed aside the waters and made a path through the sea. The Israelites made it safely to the other side.

Confidence

My problems may be big,
but God is bigger still.
When I ask for Him to help,
I'm confident He will.

I Can Trust God

I don't have a Red Sea in front of me, but I do have a few problems.

What kind of soap was I supposed to use here?

With all these new responsibilities I'm learning, I can trust that God will be with me. And I know that I'll get better with practice.

If you love me, obey my commandments.

John 14:15

God's Ten Commandments

from Exodus 19:1–20:21

With so many people traveling together, Moses needed some advice to help the people get along.

Moses climbed to the top of a mountain to have a meeting with God. God said, "I love My people, and I have a few rules that I want them to follow."

He gave them 10 rules called the Ten Commandments. Moses said, "God's commandments tell us what we should and shouldn't do so that we can live in happiness and peace with each other."

The people thought about it and replied, "We love God and want to do what's right."

Justice

I follow the rules God has given.
I know they're for my good.
They help me to be loving and fair
and worship God like I should.

For My Own Good

Here are the 10 rules that God gave:
Don't have any other gods.

Don't make any idols.
Use God's name respectfully.
Take a rest day every week.

Obey your parents.
Don't kill others.
Love your husband or wife faithfully.

You shouldn't steal.
Always tell the truth.
Be happy with what you have.

Serve [God] with your whole heart and a willing mind.

1 Chronicles 28:9

A Noisy Battle

from Joshua 6

There was a city called Jericho in the land that God promised to the Israelites. But it was filled with people who did not please God.

"I have a plan for you to capture Jericho!" God told Joshua, who was now the new leader. "March around the city walls for six days without a sound," God instructed. "On the seventh day march around it seven times, and then make all the noise you possibly can."

That sounded like a crazy way to fight a battle, but Joshua was willing to do things God's way. "Do exactly what God said," Joshua told the people.

CLANG! BANG! TOOT! SHOUT! The walls tumbled down. Now the Israelites could walk into Jericho boldly. God's way is always right.

Willingness

I do what needs to be done
whenever Mom and Dad ask.
I might not understand why,
but I still will do the task.

I'll Do It Anyway

Dad said, "Please brush your hair and change your clothes."

That's strange! It's supposed to be dinnertime.

But I did it anyway. Little did I know . . .

Pizzeria, here we come!

Work willingly at whatever you do, as though you were working for the Lord rather than for people.

Colossians 3:23

A Woman Goes to Battle

from Judges 4–5

People came to Deborah with their problems. "She stole my goat!" "He lied to me!" Deborah helped them know what was right.

At that time the Canaanites were attacking the Israelites, taking their food and animals. God told Deborah to send for Barak.

"Call 10,000 soldiers," Deborah said. "God will give you victory over your enemies." "I will go if you go with me," Barak said.

Deborah and Barak went to fight the Canaanites. "The Lord is marching ahead of you," Deborah said. The Canaanite soldiers ran away in front of Barak's army. Even their leader, Sisera, jumped out of his chariot and ran away. Later, a woman named Jael killed him as he was trying to escape.

When Deborah and Barak heard that Sisera was dead and the Canaanites had all run away, they sang a song of praise to God.

I help others out
and don't ask for reward.
When I serve others,
I'm serving the Lord.

Service

Our Secret Services

We're looking around to see where we can help or serve others.
Look! There's someone who needs help!

We made Mom and Dad's bed with a secret note tucked under their pillows.

I can do everything through Christ, who gives me strength.

Philippians 4:13

A Crazy Idea

from Judges 6–7

"God will help you chase away your enemies, who are again stealing everyone's food!" This was God's message to Gideon one day. Gideon thought: "I'm not a big, strong hero. I'm just a farmer." But he was ready to obey God.

He put on some soldier gear and got thousands of men together. "Only take 300 men, and instead of swords and spears, take trumpets, torches, and jars!" God instructed.

That sounded crazy, but Gideon was flexible and changed his plan to follow God's. That night, they blew trumpets, smashed jars, and made a humongous noise. Their enemies woke up in fear and ran all the way back to their own country.

Everyone thanked God for bringing peace. They realized it was Him and not just their noise which had secured the victory.

Flexibility

Flexible people are ready
to try something different or new.
I'm willing to change my plans
if that's what I need to do.

What Should I Do?

That's too bad. Plans have changed, and I can't go camping with my friend for the weekend.

I could cry and flood the house with tears . . .

. . . or I could adjust to this new situation and find something else to do instead.

If you need wisdom, ask our generous God, and he will give it to you.

James 1:5

The Strongest Man Ever

from Judges 13, 16

Samson was the strongest man who ever lived. He fought a lion with his bare hands as though it were a kitten; he ripped the strongest ropes and chains as if they were made of straw. God gave him great strength and courage to do a lot of good.

But Samson didn't always use his strength wisely. For example, he chose to use his strength to fight selfish people, instead of choosing to speak to them about pleasing God.

One day, Samson made one too many wrong decisions and lost his strength. Now Samson was weak and really needed God's help. "I'm sorry, God, I messed up. Please make me strong one last time," Samson prayed, and God forgave him and became his strength for a final victory.

Decisions

God can help me choose
to do what is right.
When I follow His advice,
things turn out all right.

This or That?

Play with my friend or stop to help? What should I do?
I want to make choices that honor God.

And when it's difficult for me to make the right choice,
I ask God to give me strength.

The trustworthy person
will get a rich reward.
Proverbs 28:20

Gathering Wheat

from Ruth

"We're family! I can't let you go to Bethlehem alone," Ruth told Naomi. "Wherever you go, I will go. Where you stay, I will stay." It was a long journey for Ruth and her mother-in-law.

When they finally arrived, Ruth thought, "We're hungry but don't have much money. How can we get some food?" She decided to follow the harvesters in the fields and pick up the leftover wheat. It was hard work under the hot sun all day, but she continued anyway.

Boaz, the owner of the field, noticed that Ruth was faithful in caring for Naomi. He made sure she got everything she needed. Boaz loved Ruth, and after some time, they got married.

Ruth and Naomi were never hungry again.

Faithfulness

Others can trust
what I say is true.
I finish the work
that I've promised to do.

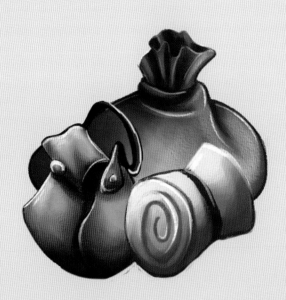

God Is Faithful

I told Dad I would help rake these leaves. But they seem to never end.

I want to get back to playing. But I also want to keep my promise to Dad.

God also keeps His promises. He is faithful and will never leave me alone.

"Hey, this looks fun! Can I help too?"

Enter his gates with thanksgiving; go into his courts with praise.

Psalm 100:4

Praises to God

from 1 Samuel 1:1–2:26

"Dear God, I'm so sad because I don't have any children. May I have one, please?" Hannah prayed. God heard and answered her prayer.

A year later, she had a cute baby boy and named him Samuel. Hannah thanked God every day for this special gift from God. When Samuel was a few years old, Hannah brought him to priest Eli at the temple. There Samuel would learn how to serve God.

Hannah would often visit Samuel. "Here is a new coat for you, my son!" She brought him special snacks and clothes that he needed as he grew older. "Thank you, Mom. They're lovely!" Samuel said.

"I thank God for you! I praise Him, for He is good!" Hannah said.

Praise

I give honor and praise to God
for caring for me.
Everyone appreciates gratitude,
don't you agree?

Everyday Thanks

Thanks for these flowers!
They will look beautiful in my room.

Thank You, God, for this food!
It will feel great in my tummy.

Just as you appreciate it when a friend thanks you for a gift,
God loves it when we praise Him. Can you count your blessings?

I listen carefully
to what God the
Lord is saying.

Psalm 85:8

Take Time to Listen

from 1 Samuel 3:1-19

Young Samuel was a good helper to God. He worked with Priest Eli at the temple.

One night, Samuel woke up because he heard someone call his name. Samuel ran to Eli, "I'm here! You called me!" Eli yawned. "I didn't call you. I was sleeping soundly. Now, go back to bed." Samuel went back to bed, but the voice called again and again.

Eli finally realized who was calling. He said, "If you hear the voice again, then say, 'Speak Lord; I am listening.'"

God spoke again, and this time Samuel knelt down and listened to God's special message.

Attentiveness

I listen carefully
and give my full attention.
I won't think about other things
till quiet time is done.

My Quiet Time

God speaks to me through
His words in the Bible.

I have a quiet spot where I
spend time with Him.

It wouldn't work too well at a
noisy basketball game or while
using the kitchen blender.

God waits for me to be
still and listen.

Do not withhold good from those who deserve it when it's in your power to help them.

Proverbs 3:27

A Shepherd Boy

from 1 Samuel 16

David was a shepherd boy who cared for his father's sheep. He led them to good grass, brushed their wool, and made sure that they were safe. David loved to play on his harp and sing to God.

At times, he was suddenly interrupted! He noticed danger creeping behind the bushes. "No way, wolf. I won't let you get near!" he shouted. "Shoo, shoo, lion! These sheep are not for snacks!"

David used his sling to scare away the beasts and did everything possible to protect his flock. "Don't worry, little sheep. You're safe again," he comforted them.

David took care of the sheep, and God took care of David. "The Lord is my shepherd; I have all that I need," he sang (Psalm 23:1).

Caring

God's love and kindness
is the best care.
Whenever I need Him,
He's always there.

I Care Because God Cares

I care for my pet dog. He needs lots of food and exercise.

I help care for my little sister. I show her how to use a spoon.

I care for my plants. I water them and chase bugs away.

God loves me and takes great care of me. I want to be more like Him.

Be strong and courageous!
Do not be afraid. . . . For the
Lord your God will personally
go ahead of you.

Deuteronomy 31:6

Facing a Giant

from 1 Samuel 17

Goliath was a giant, as tall as the ceiling. He wore bronze armor that weighed as much as a grown man and carried a huge spear. He was a part of the Philistine army—the enemies of Israel. He was so big that he scared everyone away.

Each day, Goliath came to see if anyone dared to fight him. "Ha! Ha! Ha! All the soldiers of Israel are too weak and afraid to fight me! Their God must be no good." David heard the giant and asked, "Why is he making fun of God? I will stand up for God and face up to Goliath!"

"But you're just a boy. He's so much bigger and stronger than you. You can't fight him alone!" said the king. "That's true. I can't do it on my own," answered David. "But with God's strength I can!" David put a stone in his sling. It went round and round. Goliath saw little David and laughed and laughed.

BONK! CRASH! KERPLUNK! He didn't laugh for long. God helped David to have courage and to defeat the giant with one smooth stone.

Courage

When I'm faced with problems
and fear comes my way,
I stand strong and brave.
With God's help I won't sway.

Acts of Courage

The other day, my mom and I looked through newspapers
and history books to find examples of courage.

We noticed that an act of courage
can have a big effect on other people.

There are also many ways
that I can show courage.

O Lord, I will
honor and praise your
name, for you are
my God. You do such
wonderful things!

Isaiah 25:1

Songs to God

from Psalms 8; 145

Do you like to play a musical instrument? Well, David loved to play the harp and wrote many wonderful songs that we still sing today. He wrote songs asking God for help. He wrote songs to say that he was sorry for his mistakes. But most of David's songs were praises to God.

David, who had become king, sat on his balcony to admire God's creation. He sang, "When I look at the night sky and see the work of your fingers—the moon and the stars you set in place . . . O Lord, our Lord, your majestic name fills the earth!" (Psalm 8:3, 9).

You can find many of David's songs in the book of Psalms. Here is another one: "I will exalt you, my God and King, and praise your name forever and ever. I will praise you every day; yes, I will praise you forever" (Psalm 145:1–2).

Devotion

Every day I find
a quiet place to stay,
to sing a song of praise
or bow my head to pray.

All Kinds of Ways

Like a king on a throne, I can sit on a chair and praise God.

I may not have the best voice, but I can clap my hands, dance, and cheer.

There are all kinds of ways that I can worship God. Can you think of some?

God gives wisdom, knowledge, and
joy to those who please him.

Ecclesiastes 2:26

A Very Wise King

from 1 Kings 3:3-15

King Solomon wanted to rule well, and for that he needed God's help. God told him, "You can ask Me for anything you want." Solomon answered, "God, please give me wisdom to be a good king."

God was pleased, because Solomon could have asked for lots of money, expensive clothes, and a fancy chariot. "You asked for the best thing," God said. "And because of that, I will bless you with wisdom AND with riches." Solomon listened to God's voice, and that made him wise.

We can find a lot of smart things Solomon wrote in the book of Proverbs. Here's one: "How much better to get wisdom than gold!" (Proverbs 16:16).

Solomon must have known what he was talking about; he had a palace full of gold. But listening to God and making the right choices was more important to him.

Wisdom

I ask for help to learn
everything good and right.
I listen to God and follow Him
with all my might.

I Can Learn Wisdom

I don't know the answer to my school question, but I know where to find the answer.

Now I know what to do about that. I just learned about it at school.

I don't know the answer to my school question either. Copying hers will be easier.

But when my teacher asked me to explain my answer, I didn't know what to say. "Ummm???"

101

How great is the Lord, how
deserving of praise!

Psalms 48:1

A Temple for God

from 1 Kings 4–8

God gave Solomon an important project: "Build a temple for all the people so that they can come and worship Me." Solomon worked hard to make it big, beautiful, and strong.

He wanted God's temple to be the best in the whole world. "We must use the finest wood for the roof, the strongest stones for the walls, and lamps of gold all around!" Solomon instructed the workers.

By doing their best, the people showed that they honored God. Pleasing God in the things we do and say is also part of worshiping Him.

"Dear God, this place is for You. We hope that You like it," Solomon prayed. "And now we can all enjoy expressing our love for You here."

Worship

I show love and respect to
the God who made me.
I take time to thank Him,
even when I'm busy.

What's Most Important?

I just love playing soccer!
I could do it all day long.

But I also remember to thank God
for friends, a ball, and fast legs.

We worship what is most important to us.
God wants to be most important in our lives.

Patient endurance is what you need now, so that you will continue to do God's will. Then you will receive all that he has promised.

Hebrews 10:36

The Feeding Birds

from 1 Kings 16–17

Elijah was a good man who spoke God's messages to the people. One day, God said, "Tell King Ahab that he must stop worshiping idols." This made the king upset, so Elijah had to run away and hide for a while.

"I will keep you safe and take care of you!" God said to Elijah. There were no people or food where Elijah was hiding. Every morning and evening, God sent birds to bring Elijah bread and meat to eat. There was also a cool stream of water for him to drink from.

It took endurance to wait many, many days until it was safe for Elijah to come out of hiding. Even though it was difficult and uncomfortable for him, he trusted that God had a plan.

Endurance

I persevere
till the very end.
I don't give up.
On God I depend.

It Pays to Wait

What a long wait! I feel like leaving.

Yippee! It was worth the wait.
This tastes great!

This homework sure is
taking me a while.

It feels good now that it's
done, even though it took
extra time to get it right.

109

Don't look out only for your
own interests, but take an
interest in others, too.

Philippians 2:4

A Widow in Need

from 1 Kings 17:7-16

When there is no rain, food cannot grow, and people get very hungry. This is called a famine. "Go to town and there you will meet a woman who can give you some food," God told Elijah. He saw a woman gathering sticks.

"Please give me some water and some food!" said Elijah. "But I only have a little bit of flour and oil to make one last loaf of bread for my son and me," she answered. "Don't be afraid!" Elijah told her, "God will take care of you."

So she started a fire, mixed the dough, baked the bread, and put the needs of Elijah before her own. God did an amazing miracle and rewarded the woman. Her little bit of flour and oil never ran out.

Unselfishness

I put the needs of others
above my own.
I give and share even
if little I own.

My Birthday Cake

It's my birthday! What a delicious cake! I can't wait!

I'm happy to serve my friends first.

I want to make sure they all get a piece.

No cake left . . . but . . . what a huge dessert! Wow!

Look straight ahead, and fix your eyes on what lies before you.

Proverbs 4:25

Seven Baths

from 2 Kings 5:1-15

Naaman was a soldier who could defeat anyone and anything. But there was one thing that he couldn't beat. You see, he had a terrible sickness called leprosy. "I've gone to all the doctors. I've tried all the creams and lotions they gave me. But nothing worked," he moaned. "Only God can heal that sickness!" his servant girl said. "Go and see His messenger Elisha," she suggested.

Elisha gave him a message: "Take a bath in the Jordan River seven times, and God will make you well!" Naaman was surprised. "What? Take seven baths in that dirty river? How is that going to help?"

Naaman finally did what Elisha told him to do. After one, two, three, four, five, six baths, nothing changed. But Naaman wasn't about to give up now, even though he felt a bit silly doing this. After the seventh time, he exclaimed, "It worked! I'm healed, and I'm clean, too. Thank You, God! Thank You!"

Determination

When I have a big, big job,
I don't just do a part.
I see it through to the end
and I finish what I start.

What a Job!

What a big job to clean my messy room!

It would take a bulldozer to clear out all this stuff. I give up!

What a big job to figure out this school project!

That was tricky and my hands got dirty, but I'm glad I didn't give up.

Two people are better off than one, for they can help each other succeed.

Ecclesiastes 4:9

A Wee Little King

from 2 Kings 11–12

Little Joash lived in the Temple with his uncle, Priest Jehoiada. There he learned how to walk, talk, and take care of himself. His uncle taught him about honoring God and working with others.

When Joash was only seven years old, he became the king of Israel. That's very young to have such an important job. How did he do it? "I have many things to learn, and so I have the help of many advisers," said Joash. "Best of all, I have God's help."

Joash listened to good counsel, because all of his advisers had good ideas. Some were good at farming, some were smart thinkers, and others were great builders. When they worked together as a team, they got a lot done.

Teamwork

I work well with others
without making a fuss.
We give and take advice
in unity and trust.

My Team of Friends

Building a sand castle works best
with my team of friends.

We have the diggers
and the builders . . .

. . . the decorators and snack bringers.

Don't forget someone to take
the photo. Go, team, go!

Most of the believers here have gained confidence and boldly speak God's message without fear.

Philippians 1:14

Three Brave Men

from Daniel 3

Three friends named Shadrach, Meshach, and Abednego followed God's commands. One day the king of Babylon made an announcement: "Bow down and worship my golden statue!" The three friends refused, and with boldness they said, "We only worship the true God! We cannot bow down before this idol! We want to please God, even if you don't like it."

The king got angry and threw them into a furnace of fire, hotter than any other blazing fire. But the king was shocked. "What? They're walking around in the fire, and their clothes are not even burned! Not only that, I see another man in there who looks like the Son of God. How is that possible?" The king almost fainted. "Come out!" he called. "That was incredible! Now I know that your God is real!"

The three friends were more than happy to tell the king about the true and powerful God who saved them from the hottest fire ever!

Conviction

I believe the truth.
God's Word is enough.
I do what is right
even when it's tough.

On God's Side

I learn what is true and right from God's Word.

There is some pretty good advice in here, and I tell my friends about it.

My convictions become stronger the more I learn about God.

Do what is right and good
in the Lord's sight.

Deuteronomy 6:18

Surrounded by Lions

from Daniel 6

Daniel was a good helper and friend to the king. But when the king's advisers became jealous of Daniel, they tricked the king into signing a silly rule. "Anyone who prays to God instead of praying to the king will be fed to the lions for a snack!" it read.

But that didn't keep Daniel from praying to the God he loved. "No matter what others think of me, I will do what I know is right." Daniel went home and prayed as usual.

The advisers hurried to the king and said, "Daniel broke the rule. He must be punished." So Daniel was thrown to the lions, but he trusted that God would take care of him as he stood strong for God.

That night the king could not sleep. Early the next morning, he ran to check on his friend. "I'm alive!" Daniel called. "God told the lions not to touch me."

Peer Pressure

I want others to like me
and think I'm all right.
But I don't let that keep me
from doing what's right.

128

I'll Decide for Myself

My friends are going to watch a movie that I know I shouldn't watch.

"Come on, it'll be fun," they say.

Should I go along with them?

You know what?
I'll decide to do what God wants!

129

Let's not get tired of doing what is good. At just the right time we will reap a harvest of blessing if we don't give up.

Galatians 6:9

Rebuilding the Walls

from Nehemiah 1–6

God's people were in trouble. The city of Jerusalem was in bad shape, and the walls of the city were destroyed. Nehemiah prayed, "God, what shall I do?" God gave him a plan. The walls had to be rebuilt wide and very tall. It was a huge job for Nehemiah and his helpers.

"Ha! Ha! Ha! You'll never finish it," their enemies said as they tried to stop the work. "BOOOO!" They even tried to scare them away, but Nehemiah stayed strong.

Nehemiah told his helpers, "I know that we're all tired, and we'd rather be resting in the shade. It's tough working in the baking sun, scraping our hands on these bricks. But let's not give up now. We're almost done!" It must have felt good to see the job finally completed, don't you think?

Perseverance

I keep on working hard
without giving in.
Even when it gets tough,
I do my best to win.

Strength to Get It Done

Clean all the windows?
But our house has so many!

All of the windows are squeaky clean.
There is no dirt left.

How did we do it? We began
with a prayer, and God gave us
strength to finish.

I was even able to use all my
new muscles to help Mom carry
the groceries.

You should clothe yourselves instead with the beauty that comes from within, the unfading beauty of a gentle and quiet spirit, which is so precious to God.

1 Peter 3:4

Queenly Beauty

from Esther

The king of Persia chose Esther as his queen because she was beautiful on the outside. God chose her because she was also beautiful on the inside.

One day Esther heard some terrible news. A man named Haman planned to get rid of God's people! "We can't let that happen. I will do whatever I can to save my people," said Esther. "I will go and talk to the king!" she decided.

No one was allowed to see the king unless he called for them. Esther prayed for God's help and strength, which made her beautiful on the inside. Then she fixed her hair, put on her best dress, and made herself very pretty on the outside, too.

With graceful steps she approached the king and told him about Haman's terrible plan. "What beauty and what courage," he thought. "But what a terrible plan. I'll do something about this right away." The king got rid of wicked Haman, and God's people were saved.

Beauty

Beauty's not just about
the things that I wear.
With God in me, His love
shines everywhere.

Beautiful Things

Fancy clothes, makeup, and jewelry help me to look pretty on the outside.

But a loving and kind heart that's filled with God's
Spirit makes me beautiful on the inside.

I take joy in doing your will, my God, for your instructions are written on my heart.

Psalm 40:8

Into the Fish's Belly

from Jonah 1–3

God had a message for Jonah: "I need you to go and tell the people of Nineveh to stop being so bad." Jonah replied, "Lord, I don't like the people of Nineveh, and I'm too busy." So he hid on a ship that was going the other way. "Maybe God won't find me here," he thought.

Jonah was wrong, because God knows everything. God sent a big storm with huge waves, and Jonah found himself sinking down into the sea.

God didn't want Jonah to drown, so He sent a big fish to swallow him up. Three days later Jonah prayed, "God, I'm sorry for running away and not being available to do what You asked."

God told the fish to swim back to shore, and with one big spit, Jonah was on his way. "Now I'm ready to take Your message to the people of Nineveh," he said.

Availability

I am ready to serve.
I'm available.
God can use me
as I'm able.

Who Can Help?

When Mom calls, "Who can help me wash the dishes?"

I'm available to help. I don't run the other way!

Trying to ride a seesaw by myself doesn't work very well.

It's great when others are available and willing to join me.

141

This is how God loved the world: He gave his one and only Son.

John 3:16

The King Is Born

from Luke 1:26-38; 2:1-7

Do you like hearing good news? Well, this is the best news of all. God loved us so much that He decided to send His Son, Jesus, to earth for a special visit. He knew we needed someone human like us to relate to.

But Jesus didn't come as someone rich and famous. He didn't stay in a fancy hotel or the president's house. He came as a baby.

"A bright angel told me that I'm going to have God's Son," Mary told Joseph. But first they had to take a long trip to Bethlehem. There baby Jesus was born in a manger surrounded by animals.

God's Love

God is perfect; we are sinful.
The only solution is Jesus.
God loved each of us so much
that He sent His Son to be with us.

Celebrating Jesus

Did you know that the name
Jesus means "Savior"?

I imagine a prince leaving his palace to
rescue and save someone he loves.

That's what Jesus did for you and me.
Isn't that great?

I love celebrating God's love at
Christmas. But I can thank Him
for it any time and every day.

145

I will exalt you, my God and King, and praise your name forever and ever.

Psalm 145:1

Kingly Gifts

from Matthew 2:1-12

How do you announce your birthday? Do you send out invitations? Do you put up banners or signs? Some people put up flags or even balloons.

Jesus' birth was the best news of all! God was so excited that He couldn't keep it to Himself. He announced it by sending a choir of angels to shepherds close by. But that wasn't enough, so He also put a special star in the sky.

Some wise men noticed the star. "It's announcing the birth of a new king," they said to each other. "Let's follow it! This will be the most exciting adventure ever!"

When they finally arrived, they bowed down before the little boy Jesus and worshiped Him. "You are the Son of God. We adore You, our King!" they said. Then they offered Him gifts of gold, frankincense, and myrrh.

Admiration

I'm amazed when I see
all that God has made.
I cheer, I clap, I praise.
Let's have a parade!

My God Is Great

When I pray, I show God respect and honor by giving Him my full attention.

I close my eyes and fold my hands to keep me from being distracted.

There are so many things I admire about Him, like how He made this cool splashing water for my plants.

I love the taste of these fruits. What can you thank God for?

The teaching of your word gives light,
so even the simple can understand.

Psalm 119:130

At the Temple

from Luke 2:41-52

Once a year, Joseph and Mary would go to the Temple in Jerusalem.

When Jesus was 12 years old, He came along. Later, when the traveling group headed home, Joseph and Mary thought that Jesus was walking with His friends. But He wasn't, and they couldn't find Him anywhere. "We've lost Jesus. He must still be in Jerusalem!" they exclaimed.

They looked in houses, at the marketplace, out in the streets, and on rooftops.

Three days later, they finally found Him at the Temple, discussing God's writings with the teachers. "Jesus, we've been looking all over for You," Joseph and Mary said as they hugged Him. "But why? Didn't You know that I would be in My Father's house?" Jesus answered. He was talking about God (His Father in heaven).

God's Word

I read and think about
the things that God has said.
His words are the wisest
of any I've read.

How Do I Live My Life?

Wow! Look at my new and complicated toy!

I'd better read the instructions on how to put it together.

My Bible says to "Love your neighbor as yourself." (Leviticus 19:18)

I can read God's Word to find instructions on how to best live my life, because after all, God's the One who made me.

153

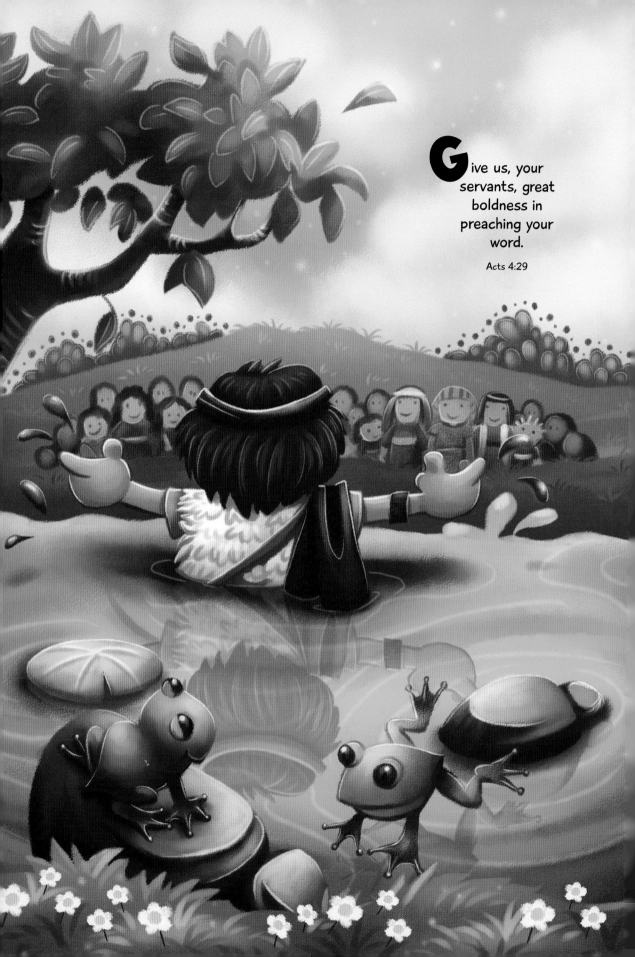

Give us, your servants, great boldness in preaching your word.

Acts 4:29

Talk about Jesus

from John 1:19-34

Jesus had a cousin named John. People called him John the Baptist. Why? Because he stood in the Jordan River and baptized people with water. Baptism is a way of showing that you're sorry for your sins and want to be washed clean of them.

John was making an important announcement: "Stop doing bad things and get ready, because the Son of God is coming soon!" Many people listened to John and were sorry. But others did not like him and said, "Who are you to tell us what to do? We can do what we like." But that didn't stop John from speaking up.

One day Jesus came to visit. "Jesus is here!" John said. "This is the person that I've been telling you about! He will save us from our sins!" John wanted everyone to know about Jesus.

Boldness

I am brave when I speak
to others about God.
I show courage whether they
boo or applaud.

The Best Ice Cream

This place has the best ice cream ever!
I have to tell my friends about it.

I know about God's amazing love for
me. I have to tell my friends about it.

When I'm bold and tell others about God, some will like it,
some will not. But it would be a shame to keep it a secret.

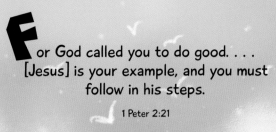

For God called you to do good. . . .
[Jesus] is your example, and you must
follow in his steps.

1 Peter 2:21

Jesus Picks His Disciples

from Mark 3:13-19

"Come follow Me!" Jesus called, and 12 men answered. These men were fishing at the lake, sitting under a tree, collecting people's taxes, or on their way to work.

They were all busy people, but Jesus had a better job for them. "If you accept and follow My teachings, then you are My disciples," Jesus told them.

A disciple is someone who learns from, and then copies, his or her teacher.

"Look, Jesus is praying. I want to pray too!" one disciple said. "Look, now Jesus is helping the poor. I want to help too!" another one said. "Look, Jesus is telling people about the good news of God's love. I want to do that too!" said a third disciple.

Jesus calls,
and I follow His lead.
I copy Him in word
and in deed.

Following Jesus

I Can Copy Jesus

How can I be a follower of Jesus? By copying Him.
I read from my big New Testament to find out how Jesus lived.

I show kindness and live in
a way that pleases Him.

He doesn't make me follow
Him; He invites me to. And I
accept His invitation!

Love is patient and kind. . . . Love will last forever!

1 Corinthians 13:4, 8

Spending Time with Jesus

from Matthew 19:13-15

The crowds that followed Jesus weren't just grown-ups. Children wanted to be with Him too. "Playing with Jesus is so much fun!" the kids giggled. "Whee! I can swing on His strong arm!" they laughed. "Goo goo, gaa gaa!" babbled the baby.

The disciples said, "Jesus is too busy for little kids. Leave Him alone!" But Jesus replied, "No! I love being with kids. God's Kingdom is for people who are like children. Don't send them away."

Jesus hugged and blessed the children. He sat them on His lap and told them stories. Even though He was very busy with teaching, preaching, and healing, through His example, He showed that love, kindness, and spending time with people were most important.

Kindness

I think of others
in the things I do.
I ask, "What would I like
if I were you?"

I Receive Jesus' Love

When I receive Jesus' love, it makes me want to show kindness to others.

Thanks for breakfast, taking me to school, washing my laundry, and . . .

Oops, my sheet of paper would never be big enough to write it all down.

I wonder how many kind deeds I can do for others today?

A glad heart makes a happy face.

Proverbs 15:13

Water to Wine

from John 2:1-11

One day when Jesus was at a wedding party, there was a big problem. The servants shuffled around, looking in every cupboard and jug. "What are we going to do? We have no more wine!" they cried.

Jesus didn't want the party to be ruined, so He told the servants, "Fill those jugs with water, and then pour a cup for the man in charge of the wedding to taste."

The servants scratched their heads, "What is Jesus' plan? To serve him water?" But they cheerfully did what Jesus told them.

As they poured the first cup, they were amazed. "Look! It's not water anymore; it's wine!" they cheered. "It's a miracle! Hooray! The party has been saved!" When the wine was served to the man in charge, he marveled, "Wow, this wine is even better than the one that ran out!"

Cheerfulness

I smile even when
problems come my way.
God gives me joy
when I take the time to pray.

I Have a Problem

I have a problem!
I lost my favorite toy.

I pray and bring my concerns to
God. He helps me to stay cheerful
until I find it.

I have a problem!
I got rained out of the playground.

I pray and bring my concerns to God.
He helps me to continue to have fun
and cheer up my friends.

169

Jesus said, "Come to me. . . . Let me teach you, because I am humble and gentle at heart.

Matthew 11:28-29

Jesus Calms the Storm

from Mark 4:35-41

Jesus and His disciples got into a boat. They rowed while Jesus took a nap after a busy day. A chilly wind began to blow, and the waves became bigger and bigger. "Water's coming into the boat. We're getting heavier. We're going to sink!" yelled the disciples as they rowed harder and threw out buckets of water.

Some of Jesus' helpers were fishermen, and they were used to big storms, but not one this bad. "Wake up, Jesus! Help! We're going to drown!" they shouted.

Jesus stood up and lifted His arms. "Peace! Be calm!" He told the storm. Suddenly, all was still. There was no more thunder, the wind stopped blowing, and the waves became calm. Jesus showed He was powerful enough to solve difficult problems in a gentle and calm way.

Gentleness

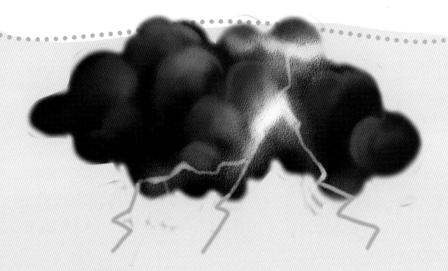

When I'm scared and freaked out,
or worried as can be,
I don't stay that way long
because Jesus calms me.

Quick, Rush, Crash!

Oh no! I'm worried that I'll miss the bus and be late for school and . . . CRASH!

"Relax, Son,"
Dad gently tells me.

I can trust God to calm my troubles. "Thanks, Dad, for a new sandwich."

I can also trust God to calm me. "Even though I missed the bus, I can have a quiet, peaceful ride on my bike."

Such a prayer offered in
faith will heal the sick.

James 5:15

Doctor Jesus

from Mark 5:21-24, 35-43

A very sad dad came running toward Jesus pleading, "Please help! My little girl is very sick! But I know and have faith that if You come and touch her, she will be well again."

When they arrived, a servant came running. "It's too late. Your little girl is dead." The people cried, "She was so sweet. We're going to miss her. Boo hoo!"

Jesus walked by and said, "Don't cry! She is only sleeping." Some people cried even more, while others laughed at Him. But the sad dad still believed that Jesus could help.

"Get up, little girl!" Jesus said, holding her hand. All of a sudden: GASP! She started to breathe. Blink, blink! She opened her eyes. The little girl was alive again! Her sad dad now became a glad dad again.

Faith

God is real, and I can trust
that what He says is true.
I don't doubt Him one little bit.
What He promises, He will do.

My Little Seed

My faith grows like a little seed.
It starts out as small as a dot.

I water it every day,
and it grows and grows.

I learn from God's Word that
He can do anything.

When I pray, I trust His promises.
After all, He is the King.

Keep on asking, and you will receive
what you ask for. Keep on seeking,
and you will find.

Matthew 7:7

A Blind Man Healed

from Mark 10:46-52

A blind man named Bartimaeus sat on the side of the road. When he heard Jesus passing by, he shouted with excitement, "Lord, please have mercy on me! Help me!" The people complained, "Oh, be quiet! You're so annoying!" But Bartimaeus shouted even louder, "Lord, help me!"

He didn't stop until Jesus heard him and came closer. "What can I do for you?" Jesus asked. "Please heal my eyes. I want to see!" Bartimaeus replied.

Jesus said, "Your faith has healed you." Ta-da! Instantly, Bartimaeus's eyes were opened. Bartimaeus followed Jesus down the road.

Why did Jesus ask what the man wanted? Doesn't He know everything? Yes, He does. But Jesus likes to hear from us about our needs.

When I need help from God
with a problem or a care,
He knows what I need,
but prefers I ask in prayer.

Asking God

God's Answers

God likes to hear about my needs.

When I ask God for things,
sometimes He answers with a "Yes!"

Sometimes He answers,
"Maybe later!"

Other times He says, "No!" But God
always knows what's best for me.

Let's not merely say that we love each other; let us show the truth by our actions.

1 John 3:18

Lost and Found

from Luke 15:4-7

Jesus told a story of a shepherd who cared for 100 sheep. "Good morning, sheep! Let's go find some green grass and fresh water for breakfast!" called the shepherd. At the stream, he heard some rustling in the bushes. Jumping into action, he swung his staff and scared off a wolf.

At the end of the day, he counted his sheep. "That's 97, 98, 99 . . . but not 100?" With a zip and a zing he left the 99 and set off to search for his missing sheep.

He looked down the path and up the hill, in the forest, between the rocks, and by the stream. "Where are you, my fluffy sheep?" he called. "BAA, I'm stuck in the thorns," bleated the sheep.

Exhausted from the long search, the shepherd freed his sheep from the thorns. "Oh, I'm so glad that I found you! Come! Now we'll celebrate your return along with the other 99 sheep."

Being Responsive

I quickly act when others
need a helping hand.
I do my best to help them
even if it's not what I'd planned.

What Could I Do?

There's a shy kid at the park playing all alone.

I'm playing with eight great friends.

God doesn't like anyone to be left out.

What can I do to help him see God's love?

A real friend sticks closer than a brother.

Proverbs 18:24

Friends Help Out

from Mark 2:1-12

Four men carried their paralyzed friend to see Jesus, who was teaching in a house with a huge crowd of people around.

KNOCK! KNOCK! No one answered. One man opened the door and called, "Hello!" But no one paid attention because they were listening to Jesus. "Excuse us, please," another man said, but no one could move because the house was too full. "Look up there!" said one of the men.

The friends climbed up to the roof of the house and pushed away some hay. They pulled some branches and moved some planks of wood out of the way. Then they lowered their friend through the hole in the roof, right to where Jesus stood.

Jesus healed the paralyzed man, and now there weren't just four friends walking. There were five friends running, jumping, dancing, and praising God together.

Friendship

A true friend will help
even when it's difficult to do.
I'm there through the good and the bad,
when I'm a friend to you.

Friends' Ups and Downs

What are friends for?
Playing games and laughing at jokes.

Picnicking or splashing in the water.

Cleaning up a mess or listening to you
when you are sad.

Helping you when you are sick.

Be rich in good works and generous to those in need, always being ready to share with others.

1 Timothy 6:18

A Boy Shares His Lunch

from John 6:1-14

Crowds of people had come to hear Jesus teach about God. Hours later, after skipping lunch and snack time, their tummies were growling for dinner. "The people are hungry. Go buy them some food," Jesus told the disciples. "But there are thousands and thousands of people! We don't have that much money," they answered.

A young boy came to Jesus and said, "I have five small rolls of bread and two fish. It's not much, but I'll share it." Jesus was pleased with the boy's willingness to share his food.

Jesus took it and blessed it. The disciples gave it to the people, and amazingly, it became enough to feed thousands. "What a miracle!" said the boy. "I went home with even more food in my basket than when I left, and my tummy is full too."

Sharing

I'll see the needs of others
and share what I can.
I'll do this with a willing heart—
that's God's plan.

Fill It Up

I have a bag of crackers.
Should I eat them all myself and fill my tummy with snacks?

I think I'll share them with a friend and fill both of our hearts with joy.

Seek his will in all you do, and he will show you which path to take.

Proverbs 3:6

Stop and Listen

from Luke 10:38-42

Two sisters named Mary and Martha welcomed Jesus into their home.

Mary sat to hear Jesus teach while Martha swept the floor. Mary listened closely to Jesus while Martha set the table. Mary paid attention to every word while Martha washed the dishes. Mary tuned in while Martha prepared the meal. Finally Martha shouted: "Mary isn't helping me with anything. I'm doing all the work! It's not fair!"

Jesus smiled. "Martha, don't be upset. Mary has chosen to sit and learn from Me. That's the most important thing she can do right now. It shows that she loves Me."

Even before a tasty meal and a clean house, Jesus preferred that they take time to be with Him. "We'll do the work together right after this."

Jesus First

Taking time with God
is first on my list.
Then I make sure that
nothing else was missed.

A Time for Everything

There's a time to work:
"I'd better get started. I have so
much homework to do!"

There's a time to play:
"Whoopie! What fun!"

There's a time to listen: "I love to hear
these Bible stories, Dad!
They help me feel close to God."

And there's a time to pray:
"Jesus, thank You for this food.
Please make it good for my body."

You, O Lord, are a God of compassion and mercy, slow to get angry and filled with unfailing love and faithfulness.

Psalm 86:15

A Wounded Traveler

from Luke 10:25-37

Jesus told the story of a Jewish man traveling down a lonely path. Suddenly . . . JUMP! GRAB! HIT! BONK! Thieves attacked, stole his money and clothes, and then left him to die.

Soon a priest passed by. "Oh, poor man! He needs help! But I've got very important work to do!" he said. He continued on his way. Then a worker from the Temple came along. "How sad. But the priest didn't help, so why should I?" He, too, kept walking on his way.

Finally, a Samaritan strolled by. The Samaritans and Jews did not like each other, but he stopped and thought, "I can't just continue on my way. I have to do something to help this hurt man!" So, with his first aid kit he bandaged up the wounded traveler, then paid for a hotel where he could get better.

Compassion

I understand that you
are feeling sad.
So I'll do what I can
to make you glad.

I Feel and I Act

CRASH! I turn to see a fallen friend.

Ouch! That must have hurt.

I act quickly: "Here, let me help you!"

When I notice someone in need,
I go and do a kind deed.

As people sinned more and more, God's wonderful grace became more abundant.

Romans 5:20

The Party Boy

from Luke 15:11-32

Some people thought that they were better than others and didn't approve of Jesus' welcoming sinners. Jesus told them this story: A father had two sons. The younger son wanted to leave home to have a good time. "I want to enjoy life, and I'll need lots of money for that!" he said. This saddened his father, but he agreed to his son's request.

For a while the son had a good time: plenty of parties, fancy clothes to wear, and delicious food to eat. But soon, he reached into his pockets and . . . "I have no more money, and now I'm hungry." Feeding pigs was the only job he could find. It was nasty and stinky work, but it gave him lots of time to think.

"I made a big mistake. Father will be upset with me, but I've got to go home." And he did. "I'm so sorry! I was wrong. Please just let me be your servant," begged the son. "What? No, you're my son, and I forgive you," replied the father. "Come, we will celebrate your return!"

Forgiveness

God forgives my sins.
He remembers none.
I, too, will forgive the wrongs
that others have done.

The Flat Tire

A friend borrows my bike for a ride around the obstacle course.

POP! PFFFFFF . . .
He returns with a flat tire.

"ARRG! GRRR! I'll never let you borrow it again!" That's how I feel.

But instead: "I forgive you. It's happened to me before too." That's what I do!

205

Be thankful in all circumstances, for this is God's will for you who belong to Christ Jesus.

1 Thessalonians 5:18

A Thankful Return

from Luke 17:11-19

Jesus met 10 men who were sick with leprosy. "Please help us, Jesus! Heal our sores!" they pleaded. Jesus said, "Go and show yourselves to the priests, so that they can see you are healed."

As soon as the lepers started walking to the Temple . . . POOF! POOF! Their sores disappeared. "This is amazing! We can go home now. Yippee!"

But one man said, "Wait! There is something I have to do first. This is important." With a huff and a puff he finally caught up to Jesus. "Oh, thank You, Jesus! I'm healed. Thank You! Thank You!"

Jesus looked around. "But didn't I heal 10 of you? Where are the others?" Oopsie! Only one remembered to be grateful and say "Thank You."

Gratefulness

Look around at all
the great things God has done.
Take some time to thank Him
for each one.

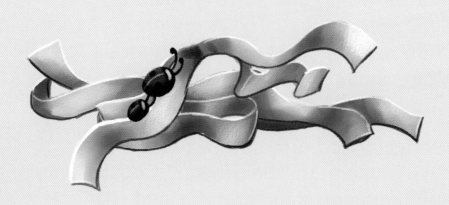

All That I Have

I have a cozy pillow on my bed.
I say, "Thank You, Jesus!"

I have shoes to run around.
I say, "Thank You, Jesus!"

Whether I have a roomful or a
handful of toys, I thank Jesus.

Whether I have my favorite food
or any food to eat, I thank Him.

209

If we confess our sins to him, he is faithful and just to forgive us our sins and to cleanse us from all wickedness.

1 John 1:9

A Changed Man

from Luke 19:1-10

Short Zacchaeus wanted to see Jesus, but the crowds surrounded Him. Zacchaeus tried to squeeze through, crawl under, and climb over, but no one helped him. But why? People didn't like Zacchaeus because he was a tax collector who cheated people and took their money.

Zacchaeus had a plan: "Here is a tree. If I climb it, I can see Jesus." Jesus saw him and said, "I am coming for dinner." Zacchaeus was in shock. "With me? Why does Jesus want to eat with a sinner?"

Jesus and Zacchaeus had a talk over dinner. "Jesus, I'm sorry for all the cheating I've done," Zacchaeus said. "I'll make things right and give back to everyone." Thanks to Jesus, Zacchaeus repented and changed his ways.

Repentance

If I do wrong, I need to ask,
"Forgive me," in words or a letter.
Showing I'm sorry always makes
things turn out for the better.

Make Things Right

1. Feel sorry:
"Yes, I ate your share of the cookies. I'm sorry."

2. Ask forgiveness:
"Will you forgive me?"

3. Make it right:
"I'll get you another bag of cookies."

4. Don't repeat the wrong:
"I promise not to eat your cookies anymore."

This is the day the Lord has made. We will rejoice and be glad in it.

Psalm 118:24

Into Jerusalem

from Luke 19:28-38; John 12:12-15

CLIPPET-CLOP! went the donkey with Jesus on its back. Into the city of Jerusalem He rode. "Hosanna! Blessed is He who comes in the name of the Lord! Hosanna!" shouted the people from the streets and the rooftops.

Some people laid their coats on the ground to make a royal carpet, while others waved palm branches. Why palm branches and not banana leaves? Palm branches represent goodness and victory.

Thousands of people danced, jumped up and down, and shouted, "Hooray! Jesus is here!" This showed their excitement about Jesus and the wonderful things that He had done for them. The people cheered and shouted louder and louder.

This was a special occasion. What do you do to show your excitement for God?

Enthusiasm

We praise our God
so all can hear.
With joyful hearts
we shout and cheer.

Yippee! Hooray!

I can be enthusiastic about God's goodness, serving Him and others.

For example, I can wash Dad's car in two different ways.

Without enthusiasm:
"This job takes soooo long, and it's just going to get dirty again."

With enthusiasm:
"I'll make this car shine like a mirror!"

217

For every time you eat this bread and drink this cup, you are announcing the Lord's death until he comes again.

1 Corinthians 11:26

Not Just a Snack

from Luke 22:14-20

On the night Jesus was arrested, He and His helpers gathered for a special Passover dinner. "I want to give you something to remember Me by," Jesus said. That's because people often forget even very important things.

He took some bread and broke it in pieces. "This bread is My body that is broken for you," He said.

Then Jesus took a cup of wine and said, "When you drink this, remember that I love you so much that I gave My life for you, to save you."

That's a lot of love! Through Communion, we remember the most amazing thing that Jesus did for us.

Communion

The bread and wine help us
remember what Christ has done.
We can ask Him for forgiveness
if we have offended anyone.

Remembering God

I have a picture of a friend in my room and a gift that she gave me. These things help me to remember her.

Jesus is someone I don't want to forget. Through this simple time of Communion, we remember His love and what He did for us.

This is how God loved the world: He gave his one and only Son, so that everyone who believes in him will not perish but have eternal life.

John 3:16

Jesus on the Cross

from Mark 15:1-39

Jesus came to earth to share the good news of God's love, but not everyone liked what He had to say. Soldiers took Him away and nailed Him to a wooden cross. Jesus loved us so much that He died on the cross for us. He was willing to be killed to save us from our sins.

Have you ever told a lie, cheated, disobeyed, or done something bad? Of course, we all sin and make mistakes. We deserve a huge punishment for doing wrong. Because Jesus loves us so much, He suffered and died on the cross to take our punishment for us.

Do you remember the story of Adam and Eve and how sin separated us from God? Well, Jesus made it possible for us to be close to God again. Isn't that great?

Salvation

I was rescued when Jesus
died on the cross for me.
He took away my sins.
I'll be with Him eternally.

A Special Prayer

Dear Jesus, I thank You for loving me so much that You died for my sins.

I accept You as my Savior. Please be my special friend.

He isn't here! He is risen from the dead, just as he said would happen.

Matthew 28:6

He Is Risen

from Matthew 28:1-10; 1 Corinthians 15:6

Jesus died and was put in a tomb with a huge rock and guards in front of it. How sad! BUT . . . that's not the end of the story! Three days later, Jesus came back to life again.

Here's what happened. At sunrise God shook the ground. The guards' knees rattled, and they fainted in fear. Then an angel rolled away the rock. Two women looked inside of the now open tomb and yelled, "Oh no! Where did He go?" The angel said, "He isn't here!"

From behind them, someone called their name. "It's Me!" Jesus said. "I'm back." Later Jesus went to see His disciples and hundreds more. They cried tears of joy and hugged Him. "Jesus, it's You! You're alive again!"

Easter

Jesus died for us
but He didn't stay that way.
He came back to life
and is our Savior today.

God's Amazing Power

Wow! Jesus was stronger than death.
That's pretty strong.

God's Kingdom is real and
I can be a part of it.

Today is Easter! We have a special snack, then we clap
and cheer as we celebrate God's amazing power!

This hope [in God's promise] is a strong
and trustworthy anchor for our souls.

Hebrews 6:19

Jesus Goes to Heaven

from Luke 24:50-53; Acts 1:8-11

Jesus and His disciples climbed up a hill. He told them, "Invite others to know about Me. Share this good news with everyone!" "We sure will!" the disciples said. "I must leave you now, but don't be sad; I will always be with you in spirit, wherever you are!" Jesus promised. "And while I'm gone, I'll prepare a wonderful home in heaven for you!"

After some final hugs and special messages, something amazing happened. Jesus rose into the sky, higher and higher, until He disappeared past the clouds.

The disciples stared in awe until two angels showed up. "Why are you still looking into the sky? Jesus will return someday the same way you saw Him go!" The disciples were filled with new hope. They looked forward to everything Jesus had promised.

Jesus is with me
I know in my heart.
He's all that I need.
We're never apart.

Hopefulness

My Hope Is in God

I'm dreaming about our trip to the amusement park!

I can put my hope in God, even more than in the next exciting thing.

How can I do that? By remembering God's promises and trusting that He will never let me down.

You will receive power when the Holy Spirit comes upon you. And you will be my witnesses, telling people about me everywhere.

Acts 1:8

Flames of Fire

from Acts 2:1-12

Telling the world about Jesus was a huge job for the disciples. How could they possibly do it? After all, there were no phones or Internet, and no TV or radio either. Jesus knew that and promised to give them a special gift in order to do the job in a way that was much better than all of those things.

A rushing wind blew through the room, followed by flickering flames landing on everyone's head. "A warm glow filled my heart, and I'm bubbling with joy!" one disciple said. "This is God's Spirit coming to live inside of us. I'm bursting with excitement!"

They threw open the doors and rushed outside to tell everyone the Good News of Jesus, the Savior. There were people from all over the place. And the amazing thing is that everyone heard the news in their own language. Every day more and more people joined God's happy family.

Holy Spirit

God sent the Holy Spirit
as our guide along the way.
Now I'm no longer shy.
He gives me courage every day.

What Do I Say?

I really want to tell my friend about Jesus, but I don't know what to say.

Ah, I remember. That's what the Holy Spirit is for!

Dear Jesus, please fill me with Your Holy Spirit, so I can speak boldly about You.

Now I have the courage to be a witness for Jesus.

Go into all the world and preach the Good News to everyone.

Mark 16:15

Good News to All

from Acts

"Let your light shine for others!" Jesus instructed His disciples. Light changes things— just a small amount of light makes a dark place bright. Jesus wanted His followers to help change things for the better. They remembered Jesus saying, "Don't hide your light under a basket because I want everyone to find Me" (see Matthew 5:15-16).

So how did they do it? They went from house to house sharing the news of salvation with everyone they met.

With God's power, they traveled all over the world to tell everyone about the love of Jesus. People who believe in Jesus are called "Christians," a word that comes from "Christ." They follow Jesus Christ and tell others about Him.

Witnessing

I share God's message
with those around me
and tell why His Good News
makes us happy.

The Bouncing Light

Look at what happens when I shine my flashlight onto this mirror!

BOING! The light bounces off the mirror onto things around it.

I can be like a mirror, bouncing God's love onto others by what I am, what I say, and what I do. Can you think of some ways to share the Good News?

You will show me the way of life, granting me the joy of your presence and the pleasures of living with you forever.

Psalm 16:11

Heaven to Come

from Revelation 21–22

One day, Jesus showed the disciple John something very special. "This is a little preview of the wonderful place I'm preparing for you and for all those who follow Me," Jesus said. He was talking about heaven.

John saw a beautiful city made of gold with gates made out of pearls. The throne of King Jesus is in the city, and all God's people live there with Him. They sing and praise Him all day long. No bad people can go in the city, and there is no more crying or sickness there. Everything that's sad will be gone forever.

Heaven

Welcome to the home of
our heavenly Father,
open to Mom, Dad, friends,
sisters, and brothers.

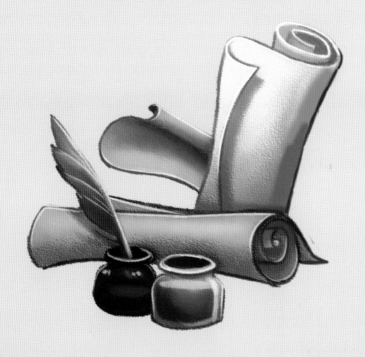

Fairy Tale or Reality?

Look at these amazing fairy tale castles! Imagine if we had our very own to live in!

But God IS making us a real one of these, in His home, heaven!

It's true. I read about it in my Bible, and God always keeps His promises.

I'll skip the plastic castle and look forward to a real one in heaven.

God did some of the most amazing things in these stories of the Bible for all those who loved Him.

He wants to be a part of your life, too. Do you love Jesus? You can tell Him right now in this little prayer:

Dear Jesus,

You are great and powerful.

You love me with Your great big love,
big enough to wipe away all my sins
and wrong choices.

I'm sorry for doing wrong. Thank You
for taking my punishment on the cross so
that I could be saved. Please come and live
with me as I learn more about You.

And until I get to see You in Your
beautiful home called heaven, I will continue
to love You with all of my heart.

I love You always,

(sign your name here)

Visit Tyndale's website for kids at www.tyndale.com/kids.

TYNDALE is a registered trademark of Tyndale House Publishers, Inc. The Tyndale Kids logo is a trademark of Tyndale House Publishers, Inc.

The Character Builder's Bible: 60 Character-Building Stories from the Bible

Previously published in 2015 as *Big Bible, Little Me* by iCharacter Ltd. under ISBN 978-1-62387-552-7.

First printing by Tyndale House Publishers, Inc., in 2017.

www.iCharacter.org

Written by Agnes and Salem de Bezenac

Illustrated by Agnes de Bezenac

Colored by Noviyanti W., Hanny A., Gabriela C., and Henny Y.

Cover designed by Eva Winters

For manufacturing information regarding this product, please call 1-800-323-9400.

For information about special discounts for bulk purchases, please contact Tyndale House Publishers at csresponse@tyndale.com, or call 1-800-323-9400.

ISBN 978-1-4964-2322-1

Printed in China

23	22	21	20	19	18	17
7	6	5	4	3	2	1